EMPIRE GHOSTS

EMPIRE GHOSTS

HISTORIC HAUNTS IN NEW YORK STATE

LYNDA LEE MACKEN

EMPIRE GHOSTS
Historic Haunts in New York State

Published by
Black Cat Press
P. O. Box 1218
Forked River, NJ 08731
llmacken@hotmail.com

Although the author and publisher make every effort to ensure the accuracy and completeness of information contained in this book, we assume no responsibility for errors, inaccuracies, omission or any inconsistency herein. Any slights of people, places or organizations are unintentional. For information, please contact Black Cat Press.

ISBN 978-0-9829580-8-7

Cover Photo of Washington Irving's "Sunnyside" courtesy of Library of Congress.

Book & Cover Design by Deb Tremper, Six Penny Graphics.
www.sixpennygraphics.com

Printed in the USA

CONTENTS

INTRODUCTION

L ong before Margaret and Kate Fox rapped with spirits, ghosts inhabited New York's landscape. The Empire
State is home to hundreds of phantoms but the spirits presented in *Empire Ghosts, Historic Haunts in New York State*
are exceptional for their notoriety and longevity. At its heart,
Empire Ghosts merges history with the mysteries of New
York where supernatural happenings furtively ferment.

*In 1848, Catherine and Margaretta Fox claimed they contacted
a deceased peddler through a series of knocks in their Hydesville,
New York home. By communicating with the "spirit" through a
series of raps, they learned his name, Charles B. Rosna. Rosna,
a peddler by trade, was murdered in the house and buried in
the cellar. The girls moved on to become famous mediums and
inspired the modern Spiritualist movement. In 1904, after the
Fox Sisters passed, skeletal remains, presumably Rosna's, were
unearthed in the home's crumbling walls.*

I grew up on Staten Island and became entranced by ghosts at a young age. I *definitely* felt reluctant to ever see one however! Fate dealt a different hand. While vacationing at Covewood Lodge on Big Moose Lake in the Adirondack Mountains, the spirit of Grace Brown manifested before my eyes. Grace Brown was murdered by Chester Gillette in 1906 and inspired Theodore Drieser's iconic novel *An American Tragedy* and Hollywood's smash hit *A Place in the Sun*. Ultimately my ghost story appeared on *Unsolved Mysteries*. The spirit encounter inspired *Adirondack Ghosts* and sparked a new career chronicling ghost stories.

Some assert ghosts are caught in a nether land; they are confused beings who don't realize they're dead, a familiar flaw among ghosts. In the following stories, such could be the case with 21-year-old Malinda Van Horn who died when a tree limb struck her head. The same could be said for George Fykes, a soldier killed in His Majesty's Service at Fort Ontario.

Some spirits stay behind out of a sense of duty like the watchful soldiers in Youngstown, an unknown soldier at West Point or the State Capitol's night watchman.

Ghosts and lighthouses seem to be a perfect fit. In New York State, a few lonely keepers remain watchful. Dunkirk, Execution Rocks and Fire Island lighthouses helped to navigate the living, now their not-so-dead keepers linger as steadfast spirits who refuse to leave their posts.

At certain hotels, some guests check in but don't check out. Several spirits stick around to show their displeasure with changes in the environment such as the White Inn's unhappy Isabel or the spirits still lodged at the Shanley Hotel. There are contented ghostly guests too like Tuxedo Man who chats it up at Hotel Utica or the convivial phantoms at the Otesaga Hotel.

Some events are imprinted on the environment and materialize over and over intensifying as witnesses react to them, like Washington Irving's spirit at his beloved Sunnyside, a Revolutionary revenant at Raynham Hall or Buffalo Central Terminal's spectral commuters.

Paranormal investigators continue to mine the mysteries at these eerie, landmark locations—in some cases, their encounters with spirits triggered personal transformation. To this I can attest.

True hauntings exist in an unknown realm. Scientific advances, especially in the field of near-death experience and research into consciousness inches closer to solving supernatural secrecies. One thing remains certain, the paranormal continues to fascinate believers and suggests our energetic essence carries on somehow in a non-physical, invisible dimension.

> *"My people too were scared with eerie sounds,*
> *A footstep, a low throbbing in the walls,*
> *A noise of falling weights that never fell,*
> *Weird whispers, bells that rang without a hand,*
> *Door-handles turn'd when none was at the door,*
> *And bolted doors that open'd of themselves."*
> —ALFRED TENNYSON, *THE RING*

New York State Capitol

State Street & Washington Avenue

ALBANY

The centerpiece of Empire State Plaza is the majestic New York State Capitol, the seat of New York State government. The red-towered building boasts hundreds of arched windows and, unlike most capitol buildings, lacks a traditional dome roof. Completed in 1899, the French Renaissance style building emulates the architectural tradition of medieval cathedrals. Decorated with vaulted ceilings and intricate stonework, the "Million-Dollar Staircase," is the structure's masterpiece. The stairway is decorated with stone carvings which depict caricatures of famous politicians, writers and self-portraits of the craftsmen. Purportedly a fruit vendor leapt to his death from the staircase. People report an inexplicable coldness on the stairs and some even witnessed a male apparition plummet to his death.

Artist William Morris Hunter created murals for the Assembly Chamber which were lost due to disintegration of the stone panels on which they were painted. Scholars say this loss deepened Hunt's depression leading to his suicide by drowning in a New Hampshire pond. Some say his angry presence haunts the chamber. Furtive shadows, flickering lights and inexplicable cold spots are attributed to his spirit.

On March 29, 1911, a horrific fire erupted in the building and consumed the western section. This region held the entire collection of the New York State Library. Reduced to ashes, the reputed depository contained hundreds of thousands of priceless manuscripts and printed rarities. Ironically, the library was scheduled to move into a new space across the street.

A 78-year-old Civil War veteran, Samuel Abbott, became the only fatality. The elderly watchman's body was recovered several days later on the fourth floor just feet from a door through which he might have escaped. (Abbott's wife Jane, died earlier in the year on January 1). Witnesses say Abbott tried to open windows in an attempt to save precious records from the raging blaze. 106 years after Abbott's death, Governor Andrew Cuomo signed legislation to install a plaque depicting Abbott and citing his service.

After the capitol was rebuilt, sounds of jangling keys, rattling doorknobs and doors shutting led many to believe the ever-faithful watchman remained on the job. One employee demanded a change in shift due to her terror. Others reported mops floated in the hallways and the telephone switchboard lit up and beeped even when calls weren't coming in.

During a late-night séance moderated by a psychic medium the spirit identified itself as Abbott. Some surmise Abbott's official recognition may allay the haunting activity but I sense Abbott's spirit will remain on the job.

Buffalo Central Terminal

495 Paderewski Drive

BUFFALO

A t the turn of the 20th century, Buffalo was the second-largest city in New York State and the tenth largest city in the United States. The first city with electric street lights, powered hydroelectrically by Niagara Falls, Buffalo hosted the 1901 World's Fair and boasted an elaborate 17-story art deco style railroad station—the Central Terminal, a jewel on the crown of the Queen City.

In 1929, Buffalo reveled in its heyday and constructed the architectural masterpiece which operated as one of the country's busiest train stations for 50 years. Centrally located between New York City and Chicago, the 61-acre complex includes a main concourse, a 17-story office tower, a four-story baggage building and a two-story mail building along with the train concourse.

The terminal sheltered individuals whose emotions ran the gamut from utter joy to sheer sadness for those either arriving home or departing. Some attribute the strength of these emotions to the haunting activity at the forsaken station.

After World War II, train travel declined and in 1956, titleholder New York Central, sold the station. In 1979, Amtrak abandoned the terminal for a newer station. In 1997, the Preservation Coalition of Erie County bought the abandoned building for $1 and formed the Central Terminal Restoration Corporation. The corporation works to restore and re-purpose the complex. In 2003, the terminal opened for public tours.

During World War II many serving in the military never returned. It's believed some of these individuals are among those who haunt the Central Terminal's cavernous halls. Are they perpetually trying to find their way home? Volunteers sense the presence of long-gone beings—some of whom expired in the terminal and/or found a resting place in its vast confines. Spooky manifestations include shadow figures actively roaming the location and disembodied voices echoing throughout the building. One volunteer spotted the apparition of two people dressed in vintage clothing standing at a water fountain in a third-floor office space. As he moved closer to see better, the people and the water fountain vanished.

In 2010, *Ghost Hunters Halloween Live* aired from the terminal broadcasting a six-hour Halloween paranormal investigation of the architectural icon. TAPS, the Atlantic Paranormal Society, utilized state-of-the-art equipment to explore the station's damp, dark nether regions. During the ghost hunters' investigation, they queried the resident spirits who responded with a blaring boom.

Electronic voice phenomena (EVP) are sounds recorded electronically and interpreted as spirit voices. Hundreds of EVPs were captured along with the sound of trains arriving/ leaving the station. An inexplicable drop in temperature is the most common anomaly reported throughout the terminal, especially on the train platforms. These cold spots indicate paranormal activity. Are the spirits still waiting for their train to arrive?

Beyond Ghosts is an organization that conducts public, on-site ghost hunts and donates some of the proceeds to support restoration efforts at the Central Terminal.

USS The Sullivans

1 Naval Park Cove

BUFFALO

The five Sullivan brothers felt themselves invincible as long as they stuck together. Albert, Francis, George, Joseph and Madison Sullivan were born in Waterloo, Iowa, between 1914 and 1920. During World War II they enlisted in the U. S. Navy on the condition they serve on the same ship. Even though this went against naval policy, all five brothers were stationed on the USS *Juneau*.

Four of the Sullivan brothers died when a Japanese torpedo struck their cruiser on Friday, November 13, 1942. For the next few days, the eldest and only surviving brother, George, swam from life raft to life raft desperately searching for his deceased brothers. A shark attacked the delirious man as he attempted to reach land.

Citizens became outraged over the incalculable loss. Never again would the Navy station family members together in a war zone.

The Navy honored the five men by christening a new destroyer USS *The Sullivans* on February 10, 1943. The vessel is unique for several reasons. This was the first time the Navy used the word "the" in the name of a ship, shamrocks adorn the smokestack and five sailors who never set foot on the craft haunt it. In 1978, the Navy donated the destroyer to New York State thereby establishing a memorial in the Buffalo and Erie County Naval & Military Park.

Workers aboard the retired ship say the spirits of the five brothers make themselves known in some way every Friday the 13th. Five luminous forms float down passageways, disembodied voices whisper "Hey, you!" and sounds of men playing cards are audible.

The terrible specter of George, the oldest Sullivan brother, his charred face and clothes stained with blood, floats above the deck. One worker quit his job when George's disfigured torso approached him at a fast rate of speed.

When photos are taken of the portrait of the five brothers, George's image oftentimes appears as a white blur. Sometimes cameras refuse to function near the painting yet operate perfectly elsewhere. Caretakers find locked doors unlocked, items fly across rooms and radar becomes activated when no electrical power exists.

Perhaps George's guilt of not being able to rescue his brothers keeps him earthbound. Or maybe he remains behind desperately seeking his brothers, as he did in the days before his death.

Van Horn Mansion

2165 Lockport Olcott Road
BURT

B orn in New Jersey, Judge James Van Horn decided to head north as the Erie Canal underwent construction. He settled in Newfane in 1817 with his nine children and built the first gristmill along Eighteen Mile Creek. The next year the British torched the mill burning it to the ground during the War of 1812.

Undaunted, Van Horn rebuilt the mill and erected a sawmill five years later along with a log cabin for his family. Business flourished and in 1823, James erected a store, distillery and an imposing brick home—today's Van Horn Mansion. Yet another fire destroyed the gristmill but James restored the structure and went on to construct a woolen factory completed in 1842.

Eventually his two sons managed some of the properties. James Jr. took over the mill operation and Burt oversaw the house and farm. The hamlet of Burt is named after Burt Van Horn.

Burt Jr. remodeled the brick mansion in 1900 by building an addition and installing the leaded stained glass dome. The manse includes 16 rooms and five bathrooms.

Over the years, the house exchanged hands many times and served as a restaurant and an apartment house. Noury Chemical owned the property for ten years. During their residency, employees spotted lights moving inside the house yet investigators found no cause. Noury donated the mansion to the Newfane Historical Society in 1987.

The old manse suffered when vandals smashed its doors and windows as it stood vacant—*or was it?*

In 1837, James Jr.'s wife, Malinda, died at twenty-one years of age when a tree limb struck her dead. Interred on the grounds, her spirit remains at her mortal abode. Malinda sightings are frequent. A female is often spotted looking out the window when the house is unoccupied. When a roofer spotted her face staring out the windowpane he almost fell off his ladder. As workers hung wallpaper during restoration, Malinda's spirit stood watching them. Visitors outside the dwelling attest to hearing someone tapping on the windowpane.

Another clue to a resident ethereal presence is the behavior of dogs inside the house. Animals are accurate barometers when it comes to the supernatural. In the Van Horn mansion, dogs bark, growl, raise their hackles and refuse to enter the library.

Spectral Malinda likes to pose in the street or sidewalk in front of her house as she did when alive. There are those who avoid driving by the mansion for fear of catching a glimpse of her ghost, some even drive miles out of their way to circumvent passing the haunted dwelling. In the past, certain drivers swerved to avoid hitting a female who suddenly appeared then just as quickly vanished.

Some sighted Malinda's full-bodied apparition claiming her spirit manifests as a mist then slowly morphs into a female form. She lingers for several seconds then suddenly disappears. Malinda's spirit is harmless but an otherworldly encounter with her is a memorable experience.

Smalley's Inn

57 Gleneida Avenue
CARMEL

S malley's Inn is a local landmark and ranks as one of the most haunted restaurants in the United States. Originally opened in 1852 as Smalley's House, James J. Smalley operated the hotel and tavern. A 1924 fire consumed the building along with much of downtown Carmel. Most of the buildings were rebuilt. Fifty years later, another blaze destroyed Smalley's as well as other businesses. Once again, Smalley's arose from the ashes.

For years, all associated with the popular eatery, commented on inexplicable sightings and unexplainable happenings. Years ago, owner Anthony Porto Jr. unearthed a girl's tombstone buried under the basement steps. A section of the underground room served as a morgue when James Smalley, in his position as sheriff, functioned as the county coroner as well. The grim discovery triggered peculiar events such as, on one occasion, every cell phone and landline started ringing at exactly the same time, each call originating from an in-house phone. Sightings of a little girl's apparition became frequent and individuals felt as if a child tugged on their clothes. Witnesses spotted ghostly figures of a man and a woman in addition to the little girl.

Paranormal investigators, using an Ouija board, identified the ghost as Elizabeth Smalley, James Smalley's daughter who died when a toddler; no one has yet to identify the adult spirits.

The inn's staff members undergo their haunted happenings most often in the kitchen and basement. Pots, pans and utensils create a cacophony in the kitchen but when checked to see what's going on, investigators find nothing amiss. Footsteps resound when individuals are alone in the eatery. Most avoid the basement because they feel a strange presence. Support pillars exist down below and Elizabeth's spirit enjoys hiding behind the columns. She peeks around them from time to time, as if playing peek-a-boo. Her startling presence frightened more than one workman, some of whom refuse to return.

In 2012, the Travel Channel filmed an episode of *The Dead Files* at Smalley's. Psychics, mediums, clairvoyants or "sensitive" individuals possess the ability to identify and make contact with spiritual entities. The show's psychic medium, Amy Allan, perceived a banshee, a female spirit commonly thought to presage death, along with a ghostly soldier haunting the inn.

Cohoes Music Hall

58 Remsen Street

COHOES

"She came on like a meteor, but there is a lasting quality. What is that quality? Radium? Electricity? Sheer nerve? Or, as Eva Tanguay herself comically suggests, madness?"

—ASHTON STEVENS, *CHICAGO EXAMINER*, 1911

Cohoes Music Hall hosts a wide variety of performances from traditional theater to rock concerts and movie screenings. Built in 1874, the four story structure is the fourth oldest operational Music Hall in the nation. The building, first named the Central Hall Block, featured a first floor post office and three large stores. The second floor held eight offices, a telegraph office, music studio and school. The music hall existed on the third floor.

The Palace Performing Arts Center Inc. manages the 475-seat playhouse situated in the heart of the Spindle City's historic district. The décor is 19th century French renaissance style in pearl and gold. Vaudeville shows, featuring a variety of entertainment, became popular in the 1890s. Most performers began their careers in small cities and towns before taking off for the Big Apple. Many luminaries performed here—Buffalo Bill Cody, George M.

Cohan, Lillian Russell, John Phillip Sousa, Jimmy Durante, Sarah Bernhardt and hometown girl Eva Tanguay.

Although self-admittedly lacking in talent, Canadian-born entertainer Eva Tanguay (1878–1947) became a brilliant Vaudeville star and performed in the 1909 Ziegfeld Follies. What she lacked in talent she made up for in personality. Eva knew how to work a crowd. Considered "the first Rock star," newspapers regularly reported scenes of fan frenzy at her appearance. At the height of her stardom, the performer out-earned stellar entertainers such as Al Jolson, Harry Houdini and Enrico Caruso.

Raised in Cohoes, Eva began her show business career as a teenager performing at the local music hall. Legend says the audience booed her off the stage during her first appearance. She became known as the "I Don't Care" girl after her signature song which is available for listening on YouTube. The entertainer possessed a risqué style, (she relished showing more than a little knee), and a scandalous reputation. Edward Bernays, Sigmund Freud's nephew and father of public relations, called her "our first symbol of emergence from the Victorian age." Rumor says she enjoyed an affair with the Cohoes' mayor before he married and they remained close friends all their lives. Perhaps this is why Cohoes became a regular stop on her performance circuit.

After a long, successful career, Eva passed away penniless in Hollywood. Today the Music Hall's performers and production crew allege Eva's spirit came home to Cohoes where she still seeks the limelight. Cast members agree a palpable presence exists in the theater. Inexplicable noises, wafts of cold and the distinct scent of perfume—all these anomalies support the notion the showplace is haunted. Several report the sound of high heels clicking back and forth across the empty stage. Sometimes a childish giggle follows. Is this Eva's spirit setting nerves on edge?

Management regularly finds lights ablaze after shutting down the theater for the night. Mysterious orbs appear in photographs taken of productions, usually surrounding the leading ladies. Props go missing right before a performance then mysteriously reappear. Most feel the culprit is undoubtedly Eva because astoundingly her specter is sometimes spotted sitting in the audience and/or opera boxes watching performances. One dowser determined a spirit occupied seat 108!

Eva's postmortem role mimics how she performed in life—engaging, playful, unpredictable but most of all memorable.

Otesaga Hotel

60 Lake Street
COOPERSTOWN

O tesaga is the Iroquois word for "meeting place" and, appropriately, sociable spirits congregate at this grand dame resort. Built by Edward and Stephen Clark, the imposing Federal-style structure began welcoming guests in 1909. The luxury hotel boasted a telephone in every room and central heating controlled by individual thermostats. These special features, combined with a stunning location on Lake Otsego's southern shore and a world-class golf course, made the Otesaga a popular destination for the well-to-do. It seems however, a couple of guests, and throng of unruly children, stay way past check out time.

The wait staff say several times a year they clearly hear someone call them by name. Alertly responding they find no one there. The ethereal culprit is a woman whose voice is soft and even-toned however a phantom male sometimes summon them. This anomaly usually occurs at dusk near the dining room and is always accompanied by an icy chill.

One waitress approached a guest on the veranda to take their order, Diverting her attention briefly to pull the server book from her apron, when she looked up her customer had vanished. In a flustered panic, she raced to tell her co-workers.

Both staff and guests report many unusual experiences suggesting multiple spirits linger here. On the fifth floor, sounds of children running down the hallway are bothersome and oddly occurs when no children are present. Another common experience is the sound of furniture being moved or slid across the floor above. When guests inquire about the ruckus, they are informed a sixth floor does not exist, nor an attic, there's only the roof overhead. Another fifth floor guest observed a person moving toward him in the hallway. As they approached each other the stranger suddenly dissipated.

On the third floor one guest sighted a partial apparition disappear into the bath. Another lodger heard moaning and crying during the night necessitating a staff member to investigate the sound. The wailing seemed to emanate from a linen closet but no source for the sounds was found.

The Otesaga operated as the Knox School for Girls from 1920 to 1954. Sights of ghostly children playing, giggling and calling people by name, especially in rooms 307 and 585, led Syfy's *Ghost Hunters* to investigate. They confirmed "friendly spirits" exist here. Guests sometimes call the front desk late at night to complain about errant juveniles running up and down the hall. Hotel clerks investigated every floor but the spectral kids went undetected.

Often, tinkling music, like a music box tune, wafts throughout the second floor, its source unknown. The ghost hunters used flashlights and a music box as a trigger object to entice the ghosts to interact. When the music played, the flashlight turned on and off. Their decoy worked!

On the fifth floor, ghost hunters used a laser grid to detect movement via light patterns. A figure actually showed up moving through the grid! In the hallway, a full-bodied shadow emerged, stared at the investigators and then vanished.

The *Ghost Hunters'* team presented evidence to support the hotel's paranormal claims. Be assured, however, there is nothing to fear from the ephemeral guests who revisit the inn they enjoyed when on earth.

1890 House Museum

37 Tompkins Street
CORTLAND

C. F. Wickwire Residence, Tompkins Street, Cortland, N. Y.

19th century industrialist Chester Franklin Wickwire built a lavish home for his wife Ardell and their two sons. The residence features towers, turrets, gables and windows of all shapes and sizes combined to create a castle-like design.

Chester and his brother Theodore attained their riches through hard work, ingenuity and a little luck. While running a hardware store, the Wickwires obtained a loom through bartering with a customer. Charles modified the device to weave wire into a form of cloth. The wire cloth later morphed into door and window screens. High demand for screening led the brothers to open a successful factory.

After the deaths of Chester and Ardell, their house remained empty from 1915 to 1923, at which time their son Frederic moved into the house and massively renovated. His family remained in the home for 50 years until Frederic's wife Marion passed away. The house and its contents were auctioned and a generous donation allowed the Landmark Society of Cortland County to purchase the home and restore the place to its original decor.

Today the 1890 house, where six members of the Wickwire family died, operates as the Museum and Center for Victorian Arts. Many believe the family still haunts their earthly abode. Property manager Michelle Grimes attests to strange goings-on. Once a heavy binder crashed to the floor in Michelle's office—without cause. Other anomalous activities include knocking, doors opening and closing and furtive shadows. The spirits who lurk here continue to enjoy billiards as well. Voices heard include a command to "Get out of here!" The interactive spirits not only talk they even touch some of those who visit the museum. Most astonishing is Ardell's full-bodied apparition moving throughout the house.

Residence of C. F. Wickwire, Cortland, New York.

Syfy Channel's *Ghost Hunters*, The Atlantic Paranormal Society (TAPS), investigated the 1890 House. Two team members discerned movement in the attic and others captured the sound of a pool stick hitting a ball on the billiard table! The investigators received a positive response when they asked the spirit to tap on the glass. In the basement, the temperature dropped and TAPS heard strange shuffling sounds; above them they hear furniture moving. Racing upstairs, they find nothing out of place.

In the autumn, the museum offers "Spirits in the Castle" tours. In the past, people who spent the night in the house heard strange noises they attribute to ghosts. This renders the special tour *especially* spooky.

Dunkirk Lighthouse

1 Point Drive North
DUNKIRK

Situated on a 20-foot bluff, the current square tower and attached dwelling is the second lighthouse on Point Gratiot. In 1826, the first lighthouse, fitted with a Fresnel lens from Paris, was erected. In 1876, the current 61-foot stone tower and Victorian residence were constructed.

The lighthouse overlooks the site of four shipwrecks, most notably, the wreck of the *Erie*. The steamship *Erie*, carrying 340 German and Swiss immigrants bound for Chicago, caught fire and sank off Dunkirk the night of August 9, 1841—around 150 lives were lost.

A young boy's apparition dressed in period clothing wanders the property. The boy's spirit tugs on visitors' clothing, as a child would do. Disembodied footsteps are audible and certain objects move, especially toys like a ball or doll. The staff feels the spirit boy is one of the children lost in the 1841 disaster.

Dunkirk Lighthouse keepers are a dedicated lot. Ever faithful, they patrol the grounds interdimensionally. Staff say a shadowy figure moves about the property. Incorporeal footsteps resound on walkways and throughout the beacon, especially on the tower stairs. The tower stairway is the most commonly haunted spot in old lighthouses because the energy expended climbing the stairs leaves an imprint. Stairways are energy pathways and somehow the stored energy releases causing the sound of phantom footsteps repeating over and over again. Who or what causes the sound of voices in the lantern room however?

Other haunting activity includes a chilly presence who staff believes is the spirit of a 19th century caretaker. Henry Severance served as keeper in 1872. A little girl sighted his apparition in the house and later recognized him from a photo. Sometimes it's challenging to take photos in the residence because unknown forces render cameras inoperable. Also in the keeper's house, indiscernible voices are heard and sometimes noises sounding like a party can be perceived.

The alarm in the main house blares without reason and windows open on their own. Oddly, furniture is found moved closer to the window. For instance a highchair bearing a doll and a rocking chair are repositioned as if someone wants to look outside. One docent felt somebody lean against him as he looked out the window in the dining room where silverware laid on the table also shifts on its own. Eerie.

The lighthouse museum offers public tours throughout the day and reservations are available for private ghost investigations at night.

Fire Island Lighthouse

FIRE ISLAND

*"Seeing a ghost is like the flicker of a candle,
just a shifting of shapes in the light and it's
gone before you can even speak the word."*
—TODD ATTEBERRY

The Fire Island Lighthouse is a well-known Long Island landmark. The historical building is haunted by a caretaker who oversaw the demolition of the original lighthouse and construction of the current one.

The first lighthouse went up in 1825; the foundation exists a few steps from the present black-banded light completed in 1858. Throughout the reconstruction, the lighthouse keeper resided in a nearby shack. Living conditions were harsh. During the brutal winter, his daughter died after she fell ill. The keeper summoned a doctor but he arrived too late to treat her. The caretaker's wife attended their daughter's funeral in Sayville but the keeper needed to stay behind to keep the light lit for transatlantic ships sailing into New York Harbor. The light went out one night and locals arrived to investigate. They found the keeper's body hanging from a rope.

Visitors report seeing the keeper's apparition pacing about the lighthouse with rope in hand. Incorporeal footsteps echo on the stairway along with the sound of his maniacal laughter. Spiral stairs have gained a ghostly reputation through their appearance in films such as the 1946 noir thriller *The Spiral Staircase* and the chilling psychological ghost tale *The Haunting* (1963). Unaccountable cold spots, indicators of paranormal or spirit activity, persist throughout the light signaling a ghostly presence.

Supernatural accounts of heavy doors slamming are baffling; no wind is strong enough to blow the heavy portals open. No one can explain this anomaly. Another oddity is windows sometimes open on their own when normally a pole hook is required to reach them.

Centuries before Fire Island became a popular destination, pirates and wreckers roamed the mysterious island—along with the ghosts of their victims. Although not directly attributable to the haunting activity here, a further eerie occurrence is the appearance of human skulls and other skeletal parts washing ashore on the property. The bones are thought to be the mortal remains of prisoners and slaves once confined to hellish prison ships moored off Long Island's coast.

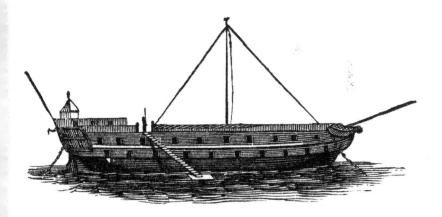

The White Inn

52 E. Main Street
FREDONIA

The White Inn, Fredonia, New York

*M*ayflower descendant, Dr. Squire White, is noted as the first medical doctor to practice in Chautauqua County. In 1811, he erected a wood frame house on the site of today's White Inn. When fire destroyed the home in 1868, Dr. White's son, Devillo, built a substantial brick structure, the foundation of the present landmark inn.

In 1918, the last resident White family member, Isabelle White, sold the property to Murray Hill Bartley and she moved next door. Bartley expanded the property and opened a 40-room hotel and dining hall much to Isabelle's displeasure. Isabelle used to watch the conversion from her porch, glaring as her one-time home underwent transformation. Most feel her spirit wanders the inn due to her unhappiness and unwillingness to release her emotional attachment to the structure. Though she favors Room 264, Isabel roams the entire inn.

Located along scenic Route 20, the White Inn is a favored destination. In the 1930s, Duncan Hines discovered the White Inn and became so impressed with the restaurant he included the inn as one of 50 exceptional establishments included in his "Family of Fine Restaurants."

Psychic mediums discern several spirits here and one sighted the full-bodied apparition of a teenage girl with outstretched arms. The oddest manifestations take place in the Presidential Suite where a huge commotion, as if furniture is being rearranged, exists. When hotel personnel open the door, all is still.

Most of the harmless haunting activity is limited to Room 264 where the culprit, suspected to be Isabelle White, continues to show her disapproval with its conversion to a guesthouse. Slamming doors and unexplained noises are all attributed to Isabelle.

In 1993, a couple staying in Room 264 experienced a ghostly visit from a teenager during the night. They described the female specter as blonde with cobalt blue eyes and a smooth complexion. The girl's spirit sat on their bed and described future highlights of their lives, including the birth of a baby boy. Fast forward… the couple returned to the inn, requested Room 264 and a crib for their new baby boy. They wanted to present their son to the she-ghost but this time she did not appear.

In 1996, a man checked in to Room 264. He shortly returned to the reception desk stating he witnessed a teenage, blond haired girl with blue eyes and a peaches-and-cream complexion in the hall. When he went to help her she vanished.

The inn's history includes the murder/suicide of innkeepers Jack and Helen Maloney. During a heated argument. a struggle ensued and Jack murdered Helen by striking her with a heavy object. He then took an overdose of sleeping pills. The intense emotion of this terrible tragedy is embedded in Room 272 and causes residual haunting activity.

Guests sometimes report the scent of cigar smoke in the "no smoking" room (Jack always smoked cigars). One couple awoke to a terrorizing racket. They heard what sounded like furniture moving and glass breaking. When they investigated the adjoining room, they were shocked to find everything intact.

Belhurst Castle

4069 W. Lake Road

GENEVA

Mystery and intrigue swirl about the ivy-covered stone mansion perched on a cliff above Seneca Lake. Long before the turreted castle was constructed, the Seneca and the Council of the Six Nations of Iroquois inhabited the property which originally belonged to the State of Massachusetts. By the 19th century, the Ontario Glass Manufacturing Company, the first glass company west of Albany, occupied the site.

At the turn of the 19th century, William Henry Bucke resided in the "Hermitage," a home built by the previous owner Joseph Fellows. He used the alias of Henry Hall, but most people knew him as Bucke Hall. Many believed Hall built a tunnel as a means of escape via the lake if authorities ever found him. Upon his death, papers revealed Hall once served as treasurer of the famed Covent Garden Theater in London. Allegedly, he embezzled theater funds, married his stepmother, fled to the United States and assumed the name Henry Hall to avoid arrest.

For 30 years after Hall's death in 1836, the property changed hands several times and eventually became known as "Otis Grove," a popular picnic area for Geneva residents. The "Hermitage" remained intact and rumors swirled the place was haunted.

By 1885, new owner Carrie M. Young Harron envisioned today's four-story mansion. She hired 50 men over a period of four years to construct the opulent Belhurst Castle utilizing materials and furnishings imported to Geneva from Europe. During this time, a workman fell to his death from the tower and a roof installer went insane.

In 1975, the property underwent renovation to accommodate overnight guests. The Romanesque-style inn boasts a four-diamond rating and a history of hauntings. The story of the spectral "white lady" is legendary and a phantom nanny and ghostly gambler keep her spirit company.

The white lady is thought to be the spirit of an opera singer who fled Spain with her paramour to evade scandal. The couple retreated to a secret tunnel to escape pursuers but the couple perished when their subterranean hideaway collapsed. Although this tale bears no basis in history, over the years, dozens of guests sighted a woman in white standing on the front lawn. Sometimes a faint, female voice is heard singing a soothing lullaby, even when there are no children present.

Dick O'Brien, a friend of the castle's owner during prohibition, allegedly died of a heart attack in the men's room. Sightings of his pale apparition add to the mystical history of Belhurst Castle.

"Behind the perception of our senses,
worlds are hidden of which we are unaware."
—ALBERT EINSTEIN

Winfield Hall

77 Crescent Beach Road
GLEN COVE

In the early 20th century, Long Island's "Gold Coast" glittered with private estates, country clubs, polo fields and marinas. Fabulously wealthy individuals such as J. P. Morgan, William K. Vanderbilt II and Alfred I. DuPont all built opulent homes, each attempting to outdo the other.

F. W. Woolworth endeavored to achieve the height of luxury with his "Winfield Hall" in Glen Cove. Marble walls and pillars, solid gold bathroom fixtures and a dining room ceiling gilded with 1,500 square feet of 14-carat gold existed among the many extravagances in the 56-room mansion. The grand staircase alone cost two million dollars in an age when money was no object.

The 5 & 10 cent store magnate made his fortune by selling household items at low prices. But the multimillionaire suffered personal tragedy. His wife, Jennie, the mother of his three daughters became mentally incapacitated. His daughter Edna, mother of socialite Barbara Hutton, committed suicide.

On the night she took her life, Woolworth hosted a party as a fierce storm raged outside. A lightning bolt struck the marble fireplace in the entrance hall, cracking the family coat of arms which adorned the mantle. The coat of arms boasted a bas relief of Woolworth, his wife and three girls. The crack split Edna's likeness, exceedingly eerie as Woolworth's daughter took her life that same night in the Plaza Hotel. Sadly, five-year-old Barbara found her mother's lifeless body the next morning.

Woolworth died only two years after the completion of the elaborate home. A known eccentric, he dreaded going to the dentist and his phobia became his demise. Woolworth succumbed to a septic infection caused by his decaying teeth.

Woolworth's brooding apparition and that of daughter Edna appeared during séances held in the 1916 mansion.

After the Woolworths moved on, the house sat empty for years. In 1929, the wife of R. J. Reynolds Tobacco Company and Reynolds Aluminum founder purchased Winfield. Afterwards, Grace Downs Academy, a women's business school, moved in. Martin Carey, brother of former New York State Governor Hugh Carey, currently owns the property.

During its tenure as a school, the house acquired a haunted reputation. In the Marie Antoinette room, people reported hearing the sounds of a woman crying during the night in the unoccupied room. A caretaker claimed to communicate with the resident spirits by tapping messages on basement pipes.

Woolworth possessed an active interest in the occult. Subtle occult symbolism exists throughout the frieze-work and other exterior/interior adornments.

The Italian Renaissance manse provides the perfect backdrop for the supernatural strains of spectral organ music said to waft throughout the spacious structure on occasion. A wispy, white mist flits through the cavernous mansion's corridors. The spirit of a morose woman wearing a faded blue gown roams the garden. She is thought to be the same wraith who haunts the Marie Antoinette room.

Burn Brae Mansion

573 High Road
GLEN SPEY

In 1907, Margaret Ross MacKenzie Elkin built Burn Brae Mansion as part of George Ross MacKenzie's estate. MacKenzie became the third president of the Singer Sewing Machine Company and confidant to Isaac Singer, the company's founder.

Upon George's death in 1892, seven of his children built elaborate summer mansions in Glen Spey. Margaret and Charles Elkin's Burn Brae Mansion remains one of three still surviving. Margaret was a philanthropist and Charles, engineer, inventor and accomplished organist, also operated a spring water bottling works on the wooded property.

Over the years, Burn Brae Mansion served as a boarding house, a tea room during prohibition and an inn. Owners, Mike and Pat Fraysse, restored the home to its original character. They currently operate the house as a bed and breakfast inn, along with a 12-room motel sited on the former horse stables.

For over four decades, guests and owners of this Victorian manse reported ghost sightings, unexplained occurrences and general feelings of an otherworldly presence. Sounds of doors opening and slamming, disembodied children's voices and balls bouncing, to cite a few. Visitors also often report the distinct sound of organ music. This is truly odd because no organ exists in the house.

Most astonishing are the apparitions of a woman in white, a man in 19th century clothing and another male specter wearing overalls. More recently, an elderly couple in their 90s, the Hapijs, both died in the house. Guests say they can still see them from the front yard playing chess by the big window, hear his classical music and smell her daily baking.

Burn Brae Mansion recently underwent restoration in preparation for its 100th anniversary. Following the renovations, the original servants' quarters, now named the Singer Suite and Elkin Room, and the adjoining guest rooms, now named the MacKenzie Suite, were opened to the public. Shortly after reopening, overnight guests began to report mysterious sights and sounds during their visit.

During an investigation, South Jersey Ghost Researchers found evidence "off the charts compared to an average investigation," according to Burn Brae's website. On a beautiful night in August, fourteen SJGR team members investigated the mansion using motion sensors, digital cameras, digital voice recorders and infrared thermometers.

Nearly 200 photos revealed anomalies as did two video recordings and five motion sensor readings. The team captured 47 occurrences of electronic voice phenomenon (EVPs) and 32 anomalous Electromagnetic field (EMF) readings. The team sensed inexplicable cold spots, pressure and emotional swings.

The very haunted Burn Brae Mansion can be reserved for paranormal investigations upon request and availability.

"When thoroughly reliable people encounter ghosts,
their stories are difficult to explain away."
—C. B. COLBY, *Strangely Enough*

Sunnyside

3 W. Sunnyside Lane
IRVINGTON

"There was a contagion in the very air
that blew from that haunted region;
it breathed forth an atmosphere of dreams
and fancies infecting all the land."
—WASHINGTON IRVING

Native son Washington Irving (1783–1859) proliferated spookiness when he penned "The Legend of Sleepy Hollow," one of our nation's best-known ghost stories. Irving based his story about the ghoulish rider on an actual apparition he heard about while tutoring in Kinderhook, New York. His characters, Ichabod Crane and Rip Van Winkle, are iconic and even Johnny Depp enhanced the mysterious Headless Horseman's global renown.

A visit to Irving's home he called "Sunnyside," is an enchanted adventure set in a romantic landscape. A gently curved path leads to gorgeous views of the Hudson River and reveals the allure of Sunnyside's unique design, intimate setting and bucolic grounds. Gentlemen docents wearing top hats and ladies dressed in hoop skirts welcome visitors eliciting a trip back in time.

The author purchased the property in 1835. Originally a small Dutch farmhouse, Irving expanded the small homestead. Combining his interest in colonial New York architecture with Scottish and Spanish structures he admired, he transformed the house into a cozy home called his "snuggery." Irving's dwelling is akin to a three-dimensional autobiography.

Nestled in the historic Hudson Valley, Sunnyside is an original, much like the man himself. The wisteria enveloped cottage houses the writer's books, furnishings and memorabilia. Not surprising, Irving's spirit inhabits his treasured estate. He became the first American writer to bring fantasy, ghosts, goblins and the supernatural to American fiction. His ethereal visage sometimes appears peering from his bedroom window facing the Hudson River.

Irving's nephew Pierre lived in the home after his uncle's death. One evening as Pierre relaxed in the living room with his two daughters, Irving's apparition passed right in front of them and entered his study.

Some say Sarah Matilda Hoffmann, Irving's fiancée, haunts a trove of trees near Irving's cottage. She died on April 26, 1809 at the age of 18 from consumption. Irving mourned Matilda all his life and he never married.

Irving's five caring nieces were the daughters of Irving's elder brother Ebenezer. When visitors leave for the day, the women's spirits tidy the house, according to legend.

A heart-broken woman, once wandered through the orchard and consumed too many green apples. She perished and stayed behind as a ghost according to Washington Irving III, Irving's great-great grandnephew.

Lindenwald

1013 Old Post Road
KINDERHOOK

The former presidential estate of Lindenwald presents a retrospective on Martin van Buren's thirty years of public service and provides an incredible insight into the past.

Originally built as a Dutch farmhouse by Judge William Peter van Ness in 1797, some of the spectral activity inside the home is attributed to his insolent son, John. An habitual gambler, John lost the property in a card game to New York financier Leonard Jerome. Although, not related to its haunted history, it bears telling that Jerome's daughter gave birth to Winston Churchill.

The sound of disembodied footsteps and doors opening and closing on their own throughout the house, reported by former residents, are attributed to John's irritation over losing the comfortable roof over his head.

Aaron Burr, Thomas Jefferson's vice-president, is one of New York's most extraordinary ghosts—his tormented specter appears in many places all over the state including Kinderhook.

Burr was friends with Lindenwald's original owner and retreated to Van Ness' estate after the fatal duel with the former Secretary of the Treasury, Alexander Hamilton. Despite the secret room's addition to the house after Burr's evasion, a long-held legend says the hidden loft housed a rocking chair, a whittled wooden pig and a faded calling card with the name AARON BURR. These finds led some to believe Burr secreted himself in the tiny cubicle during his three year hiatus to avoid public disapproval.

Nevertheless, Burr's apparition did appear in the apple orchard dressed in a burgundy coat and ruffled shirt. Van Buren's specter was also seen afoot in the orchard. Or are these visions one and the same? Hard to know. Lindenwald's orchard may be a supernatural magnet because a third ghost inhabited the grove. Not long after a despondent butler hanged himself from one of the fruit trees, his specter was sighted swinging from a limb.

The eighth president of the United States, Martin van Buren, descended from an Old Dutch family. Born in Kinderhook in 1782, Van Buren eventually became Governor of New York, New York State and U.S. Senator, Secretary of State and Vice-president. He was the first president born in the new United States of America as well as the first New Yorker to serve as president (1837–1841).

Failing re-election in 1840, the former president retired to his recently purchased Kinderhook estate to live the life of a gentleman farmer. He remodeled the home, decorated extravagantly, and named the 225-acre property Lindenwald after the linden trees that grew on the property.

Washington Irving was a frequent guest at Lindenwald and was inspired to create the character of Ichabod Crane for his short story, "The Legend of Sleepy Hollow," after hearing the tale of a headless horseman who frequented the Kinderhook environs.

According to actor and writer Bruce G. Hallenbeck, one docent shared that sometimes when they opened up the museum in the morning, they found curtains removed from the windows and some objects seemingly washed in a bucket of water.

The most delectable supernatural demonstration is the aroma of fresh baked bread or pancakes cooked on a buttered skillet. Could it be Aunt Sarah cooking up a stack from beyond the grave? Sarah was a free slave whose culinary skill was legendary. She worked at the estate for many years and ruled her kitchen with an iron first. Many feel Sarah's spirit remains attached to her earthly domain.

Heat and humidity inside the historic house museum are closely monitored and a hydrothermal graph delineates the measurements every twenty-four hours. In *Hauntings of the Hudson Valley*, Linda Zimmerman relates that one New Year's Eve the temperature spiked inside the dwelling as if warm-blooded individuals were present for several hours, even though staff found no evidence, or possible entry, of any interlopers. Now there's a New Year's Eve party I'm sorry I missed at the Martin Van Buren National Historic Site!

Lily Dale Assembly

5 Melrose Park
Lily Dale

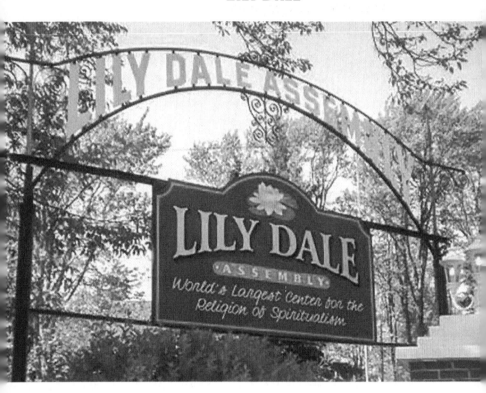

Lily Dale is the home of Spiritualism. In 1848, Catherine and Margaretta Fox claimed they contacted a deceased peddler through a series of knocks in their Hydesville, New York home. The Fox sisters took their show on the road and became international sensations sparking intense interest in speaking to the dead.

By 1855, eight million people in the US and UK followed the Spiritualist movement which stresses the continuance of life after death and asserts spirit communication is natural and entirely possible. Spiritualists eagerly engaged in various practices to communicate with their deceased loved ones, séances and table tipping for instance. Today's amateur ghost hunters can be traced to the Spiritualist era and early organizations founded to investigate paranormal phenomena, like London's Ghost Club and the Society for Psychical Research.

Lily Dale was founded in 1879 as a meeting place for Spiritualists. The lakeside commune became a mecca for mediums who communicated with the dead via trumpets, automatic messages scrawled on chalkboards and message services at "Inspiration Stump," an energy vortex in Leolyn Woods. Spirit is palpable as mediums bring forth messages. Leolyn Woods is a rare gem of remaining old growth forest in New York State. These ancient trees were seedlings when Native Americans walked the land. Visitors sometimes claim they sense the natives' spirits and some even been touched by the unseen inhabitants.

Tens of thousands flock to Lily Dale during the summer to participate in mediumship readings, entertainment, sacred music, healing services, special workshops and seminars on clairvoyance and healing. More than 50 certified mediums and spiritual healers are registered with the Assembly. All mediums must pass a stringent test to receive certification as a registered medium.

The curious also arrive to participate in the unique ghost walks offered at the Victorian haunted landmark. At the Healing Temple, "spirit lights" flicker on film as healers channel spirit to help those in need. Lily Dale's small museum is dedicated to the history of Spiritualism. Once a one-room schoolhouse, paintings precipitated onto canvas by unseen hands adorn the walls.

The historic Maplewood Hotel, situated near the water, sits as the center of activity since the 1880s. On summer evenings, the faithful continue to gather on its front porch to recount their day or quietly meditate. Originally a barn, at times the residual sound of horses who once lodged there are audible. Susan B. Anthony, Mae West and Harry Houdini, among others, roomed at the vintage hotel.

The Maplewood provides a peek into Lily Dale's past and paranormal activity is part of the package. The ghosts are generally quiet other than the footsteps heard thudding down the hall. A vanishing maid wearing a brown dress is sometimes spotted ascending the stairs to the third floor. Unintelligible, whispered conversation can be heard in the halls when no one is around. Some claim to feel touched by cold hands.

The Angel House is perched on the corner of Cleveland Avenue near the Assembly entrance. Owners Frank and Shelley Takei populate the place with hundreds of angel figurines and symbols. Spirits are tangible inside the lavender guesthouse. In fact, Shelley and a friend sighted a misty female form in an upstairs bedroom. The sound of someone ascending the stairs is sometimes heard when no guests inhabit the house. Once as a medium gave a reading the spirit communicating stood behind her. The spirit(s) is always present when communicating through a medium.

The presence of spirits is tangible all over the Dale. Spirits are everyone but none more so than at Lily Dale.

"During the prehistoric age of mankind, spirit was presumed to exist everywhere and was not held in honor as a privilege of man. Because, on the contrary, ...one saw in the spirit that which unites us with nature, not that which sunders us from it."
FRIERICH NIETZSCHE, *Daybreak*

Execution Rocks Light

MAMARONECK

Execution Rocks Light.

Execution Rock Light aids marine travel near the rocky reefs off Sands Point, Long Island Sound. The brown and white lighthouse in Nassau County stands 58 feet tall and signals a flashing white light.

The eerie name sprang from a gruesome 18th century war tactic. During the American Revolution, British soldiers abducted rebels and took them to the isolated reef where the prisoners were tortured and ultimately executed. The Brits chose the secluded spot to prevent further enmity. The cruel captors chained condemned prisoners to metal spikes driven into the rock and left them wallowing at low tide. When the tide rose, the captives slowly drowned or were ravaged by sharks. By the 19th century this brutal practice ended yet nautical charts still noted the rocky outcropping as "Executioner's Rock." The hazardous reef remained a great danger and continued damaging and wrecking ships traveling the busy trade routes of Long Island Sound. A lighthouse to mark these harmful rocks became essential.

The remote Execution Rocks Lighthouse was commissioned in 1847. Twenty years later the keeper's quarters was added. The beacon protected the island and surrounding waters without incident for the next 70 years, at which point, Execution Rock Light and its environs hosted unimaginable evil.

Before being hanged for murder, serial killer Carl Panzram claimed in a posthumous autobiography that in the summer of 1920 he sexually assaulted and killed a total of ten sailors and dumped their bodies at sea near Execution Rocks.

Boaters and fishermen claim the ghosts of the men who died on the reef, whether at the hands of their captors, victims of shipwrecks or Panzram, appear near the light station. Disembodied screams from the spectral, condemned men chained to the rocks are heard by people on shore. Because of the reef's haunted history, the U. S.

Lighthouse Service relieved from duty any keeper assigned to the remote light station who asked.

In 1979, the lighthouse became fully automated. Coast Guard members gladly gave up the night watch at the lonely outpost. With so many souls meeting their demise here, it's no wonder strange sounds and ghostly visions are experienced at the light. In fact, Execution Rocks Lighthouse was featured in a 2009 episode of Travel Channel's *Ghost Adventures*.

Former light keeper Dave Hall (1978–1979) experienced disconcerting anomalies while stationed at the post. Attached to motion sensors, a bell-based alarm system warned ships of their proximity to the rocks. Some nights the alarm bell sounded repeatedly without cause. On several occasions, as the keeper relaxed on the couch he experienced a pressure pushing down on his chest, keeping him pinned to the sofa. Dave attributed these occurrences to the spirit of a British soldier.

A psychic medium suggested an aggressive male presence haunts the lighthouse, most likely the presence of serial killer Panzram.

Zak Bagans and his *Ghost Adventures* crew heard a disembodied voice during their paranormal investigation. Their electromagnetic field meter spiked suddenly and they caught an unexplained sound. The spirit of a former light keeper attempted to communicate. The remote location and eerie atmosphere drove this early keeper to commit suicide by ingesting mercury. The keeper's ghost commented to Zak that, "hanging would have been quicker."

Morris–Jumel Mansion

65 Jumel Terrace

MANHATTAN

In 1756, British Colonel Roger Morris arrived in the colonies to fight the French and Indian Wars. He served with George Washington who became his friend. Both Morris and Washington courted heiress Mary Philipse but ultimately Morris won her affection.

He designed and built a summer villa for his wife in 1764 and named the 130-acre estate Mount Morris. Back in the day, the elevated property offered stunning views of the Harlem, Hudson and East Rivers. At the outbreak of the American Revolution, the Morris family evacuated their home and General George Washington made the property his headquarters during the Battle of Harlem Heights. The colonial mansion is Manhattan's oldest surviving house.

In 1810, affluent wine merchant Stephen Jumel purchased the estate. Jumel made his fortune in cotton, sugar, coffee and indigo. His Manhattan warehouse became the leading liquor emporium in the city where he socialized with affluent citizens such as Thomas Jefferson, Aaron Burr and Alexander Hamilton. His mistress, former call-girl, stage actress and courtesan, Eliza Brown (born in poverty as Betsy Bowen) was described as "a beautiful blonde with a superb figure and graceful carriage." Before Jumel, Eliza curried favor from both Hamilton and Burr who competed for the woman's attentions. Their mutual desire instigated their infamous duel.

Eliza manipulated Jumel into marrying her on her death-bed. She pleaded with him to make an honest woman out of her before it was too late. He married her and she miraculously recovered.

When Stephen died in 1833, Eliza became the wealthiest woman in America. A year later she married 77-year-old Aaron Burr. The convenient marriage allowed Eliza entrée to higher social circles. The stormy marriage ended in divorce a year later, the decree ironically granted on September 14, 1836, the day Burr passed away.

After Burr died, New York society rejected Eliza. Despite her remarkable climb from poverty to wealth, she lived out her life as a recluse in the mansion until her death at age 93.

The City of New York purchased the property in 1903. The fully restored abode is listed on the National Register of Historic Places and features nine period rooms and a few fantastic phantoms. Eliza is one of the restless spirits wandering throughout the house. Her apparition always appears dressed in a shade of purple, the fiery mistress is often heard rapping on the windows and walls. Curators and visitors commonly interrupt Eliza's spirit form entertaining soldiers in her opulent bedroom. Aaron Burr supposedly helps her haunt the mansion; several visitors report encountering Burr's wraith. But Eliza's first husband made his presence known as well.

Stephen Jumel's agitated ghost communicated to the late paranormal investigator Hans Holzer through psychic medium Ethel Myers during two séances. Jumel stated Eliza murdered him by removing the bandage covering injuries he incurred in a pitchfork accident and mercilessly watched him bleed to death.

Other hauntings at the manse include the ghosts of a servant girl who committed suicide after being jilted and a Hessian soldier who tripped and fell on his bayonet while hurrying down stairs. On occasion visitors find themselves among a group of uniformed men lurking about the elegant dining room.

Another bona-fide ghost is a Revolutionary War soldier who is the subject of a painting hanging in the mansion. Several docents and visitors say the depicted soldier springs to life on occasion and walks out of his large gilded portrait.

The most momentous ghostly event occurred when a busload of boisterous school children arrived for a tour. They spotted a mysterious lavender-gowned woman outside on the balcony who admonished them to *"Shush!"* The moody mistress turned and walked *through* the solid wooden door into her bedchamber. When the astonished kids entered the home they found no one *alive* inside the house at the time who fit the description of the scolding specter.

Merchant's House Museum

29 E. 4th Street

MANHATTAN

The fascinating history of the Merchant House is tarnished with sadness. Spinster Gertrude Tredwell lived alone in the family's comfortable home long after her tyrannical father passed away. Over the years the eccentric woman grew more and more reclusive and left her dwelling only under the cloak of darkness to purchase food and other necessities.

Her story begins in 1840 when *uptown* meant 14th Street where wealthy New Yorkers relocated to escape crowded lower Manhattan. The neighborhood's well-to-do residences showcased the inhabitants' wealth. Considered one of the finest examples of Greek revival architecture in the nation, the New York City landmark is a treasured survivor of the 19th century.

The decorative five-story brownstone structure served as the Tredwell family home for a century. Seabury Tredwell, a stern and hard man, earned his fortune in the hardware business. Tredwell fathered eight children—only two went on to marry. When the patriarch died in

1865, Phebe, Julia, and Gertrude lived out their lives in the East Fourth Street home, surrounded by their parents' familiar possessions.

As a young woman, Gertrude met the love of her life in Lewis Walton, a medical student. Tredwell took exception to the young man's lack of social status and decided the suitor's only interest was Tredwell's sumptuous fortune. Another strike against his daughter's relationship was Walton worshipped as a Roman Catholic while Tredwell staunchly practiced the Anglican faith. This unfortunate set of circumstances eliminated Walton as an eligible match for his heartbroken daughter.

Her sister Sarah fared much worse. Sarah so feared her father's wrath she committed suicide rather than face Tredwell when she discovered she was pregnant. An alternate version of Sarah's sorry tale relates that as soon as she birthed the child her father bribed a servant to smother the newborn. Either way, inconsolably depressed, Sarah wandered along the East River day and night in every kind of weather. She ultimately contracted pneumonia and died.

For decades, Gertrude resided in the house oblivious to changes in the vicinity and the world. She existed in the ancient house and never made any changes. In 1933, Gertrude passed away in her bed at the age of 93. By then, Gertrude was impoverished, yet she left one of the most valuable legacies imaginable—the only family home in New York City to survive intact from the 19th century with original furniture, decorative arts and personal possessions.

The treasure trove included all the family possessions—books, china, clothing, furnishings, glassware, memorabilia, an incomparable bequest. Three years after Gertrude's death, the Tredwell home opened as a museum. As conservators and interpreters carefully sorted through and catalogued the belongings they distinctly felt an unseen presence watched their every move.

The history of hauntings date to the 1930s when one worker observed Gertrude's apparition on the nearby staircase. She glanced away momentarily but when she looked again Gertrude's ghost had vanished. Another favored spot for Gertrude's post-mortem appearances is near the parlor's fireplace. Sometimes photographs taken by the hearth reveal strange and inexplicable anomalies. Many catch a chill in Gertrude's bedroom. Museum staffers sometimes discern the depression of a body on Gertrude's bed as if someone slept there the night before.

For decades, an ever-growing number and variety of witnesses, including journalists and psychic researchers, frequently reported Gertrude's spirit, wearing a brown dress moving about the house. Visitors see her phantom figure *gliding* across floors and up the stairs. Accounts of unexplained phenomena, including temperature fluctuations, inexplicable smells, disembodied voices and footsteps, sounds of parties and piano-playing heard from the street, along with the ghost sightings marks the Merchant House as the "Most Haunted House in Manhattan."

When denied the love of her life, Gertrude shut herself off from the world. The lonesome woman still won't venture forth—not even to cross over to the next world.

Shanley Hotel

56 Main Street

NAPANOCH

The Shanley Hotel is one of the most famous haunted hotels in New York State. In fact, this hostelry claims to be so frightening guests are asked to sign a waiver before spending the night!

Hotel management claims a series of deaths occurred within the hotel. The tragic history includes deaths of young children. These unfortunate events are blamed for the many reports of paranormal activity throughout the building. Guests discern children laughing and running up the stairs, doors open and close on their own and a general feeling of unease pervades the place. Paranormal investigators documented the activity with electronic voice phenomena and photos.

The hotel opened in 1845 and burned to the ground fifty years later. Rebuilt on the same site, James Louis Shanley purchased the property in 1906. Shanley and his wife Beatrice, welcomed guests which included Thomas Edison and Eleanor Roosevelt, a personal friend of Mrs. Shanley. The Shanleys suffered the loss of their three children who all died before they were nine-months-old.

In 1911, the hotel barber, who lived on-site with his family, lost his younger daughter when she fell into a well and died. A few years later, Beatrice's sister Esther died in the hotel from influenza.

It's alleged the little girl, Esther, along with Shanley's brother Andrew, haunt the hotel. Apparitions, drastic temperature changes, rocking chairs rocking on their own, clocks chiming, a phantom feline, disembodied footsteps, ghostly giggles, feelings of being touched, watched and/ or followed and objects moving on their own pretty much sums up the extent of the paranormal experienced at the Shanley!

Shanley died in 1937 and his spirit still lingers according to the hotel's website. His spirit still walks the halls, climbs the stairs and whistles.

The Shanley Hotel offers lodging, ghost tours, and the chance for visitors to get up close and personal with the great beyond.

Naples Hotel

111 S. Main Street

Naples

Designated the "finest brick hotel in Ontario County," the 1895 Naples Hotel became a destination landmark drawing many notables including radio news commentator Paul Harvey and Senator Robert F. Kennedy, when he served as U.S. Attorney General.

In the 1920s, a male guest committed suicide by hanging in a third floor room. The proprietors feel his spirit haunts the inn. The owners named their resident wraith "Topper" inspired by the 1937 movie about a couple who realize they're dead and are now ghosts. Topper is a ghostly guest who often wanders about the hotel.

"Alice" and her two children are other spectral tenants who purportedly died on-site during the 1900s. Alice usually sits in the Victorian-style dining room and her two spirit children have been spotted peering out the upstairs windows.

Two gentlemen haunt the Asian-themed room called "Sake." These remarkable spirits will respond to questions by flickering flashlights for willing ghost hunters. A lilac scent is the tell-tale sign of the presence of another long-term guest. The apparition of a resident Civil War soldier descends the basement steps at least once a year.

The eerie occurrences at the landmark inn can include bothersome activity such as one waitress's claim that an unseen hand threw an ice cube at her even when no ice existed in the vicinity. Other irksome goings-on, especially for a hotel, is doors unlock and open on their own and televisions turn on at random.

Pictures shift and objects move, voices are heard when no one else is present and a shadowy figure dressed 1920's style lurks. Only a few rooms are spirited so guests can bypass the phantom feature if they wish.

The Syfy channel's *Ghost Hunters* crew investigated the hotel in 2011. When The Atlantic Paranormal Society (TAPS) team visited the location, Grant Wilson discerned a conversation, as if three men were talking; team members also heard a loud scream. Both of these anomalies were aurally recorded. In the basement as investigators Adam Berry and Britt Griffith asked the spirits for a sign, the light fixture fell from the ceiling!

The Naples Hotel opens its doors to curiosity and spirit seekers alike to document paranormal claims.

Red Coach Inn

2 Buffalo Avenue
NIAGARA FALLS

The English Tudor-style inn with its red-bricked first floor, black wrought iron gates and steeped roof, offers views of Niagara's Upper Falls to weary travelers. When the Red Coach Inn opened in 1923, Niagara Falls was already well-established as a favored destination for newlyweds.

Niagara Falls gained popularity as a honeymoon destination in the 1800s when those with means to travel flocked to the area's famous falls eager to partake in its romanticism. By the early 1900s, Niagara Falls became the "Honeymoon Capital of the World."

In 1927, the inn hosted its most infamous couple. The newlyweds registered around midnight eager to enjoy the first night of their honeymoon. They were given the third floor Victoria Suite featuring fantastic views. By morning, the couple was dead. The bride laid on the bed, bludgeoned to death with a candlestick. The groom took his own life.

Ever since the brutal, double murder, staff and guests reported seeing a woman wearing an old-fashioned, white lace dress roaming the hotel. They've heard things they can't explain, seen things they can't believe and most attribute them to the apparition.

On *Celebrity Ghost Stories*, actor Barry Kopell recounted seeing a young woman in a wedding dress glide through the wall into the hallway. He witnessed her mutilated face. The spectral woman walked towards him "with a look of anger and accusation," as if he blaming him for her demise.

Receptionists say the hotel is haunted by the ghost of a four-year-old girl as well. Before the Red Coach Inn was constructed on the site, horse stables occupied the property. A raging blaze consumed the building and the remains of a young girl were found among the rubble. Her spirit, along with the bride's is blamed for the inn's paranormal mischief. Purses are thrown onto the floor, some guests feel brushed up against and motion detector alarms blare for no reason.

Ghost hunters use electromagnetic field (EMF) meters to look for spikes in the EMF signal. Spikes suggest changes in electrical current thus indicating a spirit being. One ghost enthusiast used an EMF meter while exploring the building, specifically to detect any fluctuations near the Victoria Suite. The EMF reading started off in the 70s and grew higher as he approached the room. On the third floor, the gadget read in the 90s. Directly in front of the suite the EMF reader spiked to 124! As he left the area, the meter dropped to normal.

Fört Ontario

1 East Fourth Street

OSWEGO

Overlooking Lake Ontario, star-shaped Fort Ontario is notoriously known for its haunted history. The British erected the fort in 1755 during the French and Indian War as a defense against French invasion from Canada. Originally known as the Fort of Six Nations, the British continued occupation throughout the Revolution. Predictably, one of the location's official ghosts is the revenant of a red-coated soldier, the typical British uniform worn at the time. Corporal George Fykes died of disease and makes his presence known by sudden drops in temperature. His phantom appeared to every new regiment for over a century. Corporal Fykes is buried on-site and is associated with a legend stating he will haunt anyone who stands on his grave. Conversely, if you jump over his grave, you can choose to curse someone of your own choosing.

On October 5, 1759, regiment officer Lieutenant Peter Penier challenged Lieutenant Basil Dunbar to a pistol duel. No one knows why the duel occurred—some say it took place because of a woman. Dunbar died of a gunshot wound to the chest. His specter appears dazed and confused as if unaware he's dead.

The fort continued to be modernized over the years and operated as an active military base until 1940. During World War II, the fort housed refugees. At this time, another celebrated spirit at the garrison manifested as a ghostly orb of light. Promptly at midnight a saucer-sized ball of light hovered over the head of the duty-guard and keep pace with the sentry for the duration of his watch. Was this anomaly the spirit essence of a long-ago soldier still on lookout? Whatever it was left the post with the fort's decommission after the war.

One of the most frequent paranormal encounters at Fort Ontario is a ghostly boy who is seen and heard crying, laughing and playing around the fortress. Recently, a picture taken of "David," the ghost boy became a sensation. The story goes an anonymous photographer snapped random shots of the fort. The next day, he gave the photograph of the ghostly boy to the fort stating he didn't believe in "this type of stuff" and wanted nothing to do with the image. Other anonymous ghosts include a headless soldier and a female spirit. In a few of the buildings, inveterate ghost hunters, equipped with electromagnetic field detectors and infra-red cameras, registered high levels of electromagnetism and captured dozens of mysterious light orbs indicating the presence of an energy source.

INTERIOR VIEW OF OLD FORT ONTARIO. OSWEGO. N. Y.

Currently, Fort Ontario is managed by NYS Department of Parks, Recreation and Historic Sites. Today, visitors experience the star-shaped fort restored to its 1867–1872 appearance and perhaps sense the leftover spirits still stationed at the remote outpost.

Raynham Hall

20 West Main Street

OYSTER BAY

John André, a British Major during the Revolutionary War is one of Long Island's best-known ghosts. He has haunted Raynham Hall, an ancient saltbox house, for over 200 years.

Raynham Hall was home to the Townsend family, one of Oyster Bay's founding families and a member of George Washington's Culper Spy Ring during the American Revolution. The home dates to 1740. In 1850, a Townsend grandson named the dwelling Raynham Hall after the Townsend seat in Norfolk, England. In 1913, Julia Weeks Cole, who first documented the ghostly goings on, purchased the estate.

At the time of the Revolution, Americans were either Patriots—those who wanted independence from Great Britain, or Loyalists those who remained loyal to King George and wanted to stay an English Colony. During the British occupation of Oyster Bay in 1778, the Townsends, revolutionists in a loyalist stronghold, became obliged to quarter British officers of the Queen's Rangers, a loyalist regiment commanded by Lieutenant Colonel John Simcoe.

Major André spent many hours at Raynham Hall conferring with Simcoe. One day as the two British officers conversed, Sally Townsend overheard them plotting about payment to Benedict Arnold for the surrender of West Point. Through their Culper spy ring connections, the Townsends managed to relay the treasonous plot to Washington.

General Benedict Arnold, hero of the Battle of Saratoga, manipulated Washington into granting him command of West Point. The strategically placed fortification on the Hudson River protected northern New York from attack. Arnold, who felt slighted for his services, plotted to surrender the stronghold to the British for £20,000. Arnold's scheme failed when André was apprehended near Tarrytown. Caught red-handed with Arnold's missive, the major ultimately faced execution. André haunts Raynham Hall ever since. (Arnold fled to England for refuge and died in London in 1801).

Julia Cole wrote in 1938 that a guest awoke in the middle of the night to the sound of a ghostly man on horseback outside the bedroom window. Cole theorized the specter belonged to Major André who visited the house shortly before his capture and execution.

Coles' sister, Susan Coles Halstead, sighted a specter descend the front stairs then vanish. Halstead positively identified the ghost as Robert Townsend, the Revolutionary War spy.

CAPTURE OF MAJOR JOHN ANDRE.

Three American militiamen captured Major John Andre carrying papers describing the defenses at West Point. His conspiracy with Benedict Arnold exposed, he was sentenced to death by hanging. Angry at both the Americans for denying his request to be executed by firing squad and the British for refusing an offer of exchange for Benedict Arnold, he died an indignant man. His ghost roams Tarrytown's Patriot's Park.

Paranormal incidents occur at or near the stairs. A museum visitor claimed to hear the swish of petticoats behind her as she walked past the base of the staircase.

She then sighted a portion of a figure, dressed in Victorian finery, go down the hallway toward the back of the house. The frequency of haunted stairways is attributed to their constant use. The energy pathways record past events and replay them as a residual haunting, like a supernatural video projection of past events onto the modern environment.

Unexplained noises resound throughout the house. Staff members hear distinct footsteps following them throughout the front hallway of the home's Victorian section. Sounds emanate from the slaves' quarters currently used for storage. Unexplained smells are common in the colonial portion where staff and visitors smelled pipe tobacco and wood smoke. In the kitchen, staffers feel the spirits like to welcome visitors by manifesting delightful aromas of apple pies baking or cinnamon.

Another spectral resident showed himself in 1999. First sighted looking into the garden from the servants' entrance, the man, between the ages of 20 and 30, wore a dark woolen coat with brass buttons. Staffers deduced this manifestation was Michael Conlin, an Irish immigrant who worked at the home as a servant in the 1860s.

Another ghost story revolves around the relationship of Sally Townsend with John Simcoe. She is believed to have fallen in love with Colonel Simcoe during his stay at the home. At war's end, Simcoe returned to England where he married. Sally remained single on the other hand and died in the house at the age of 82. After her death, Simcoe's Valentine letter emerged with well-worn creases from countless readings. The temperature in Sally's room remains about 5–10 degrees colder than the rest of the house. Psychic mediums and ghost hunters claim to discern Sally's unhappiness.

The ghost of a servant woman materialized on at least one occasion in the kitchen. She could be the spirit responsible for the delicious scent of baking apples commonly experienced.

Electronic voice phenomenon (EVP) recorded at the site by Long Island ghost investigators documented spine-tingling voices saying, "Yes, there is," "Be patient," "Yes… I am," "I'm mad at you," "Shh," and "I want outta here" in response to the researchers' questions.

Other traces of paranormal phenomena include the smell of whiskey at times and a rosy aroma wafting through the historic and *very* haunted home.

The house is owned by the Town of Oyster Bay and operated as a public museum by the Friends of Raynham Hall Museum, Inc. Raynham Hall is listed on the National Register of Historic Places, a Town of Oyster Bay Landmark and is a featured site on the Oyster Bay History Walk.

Palmyra Historical Museum & Wm. Phelps General Store

123 Market Street & 140 Market Street

PALMYRA

D oors slamming, mysterious footsteps, disembodied voices and spectral piano music are all in a day's work for staff and volunteers at two of Historic Palmyra museums. An incalculable loss accounts for most of the haunting activity.

On December 20, 1964, a fire erupted at 123 Market Street. Tragically, six young children, Eddie, Dennis, Sharon, Susan, Mitchell, Samuel and their mother, Ruth Anna Breeden, aged 25, perished in the flames. The children ranged in age from two to eight-years-old. The blaze remains the worst conflagration in Wayne County history.

Originally located on Main Street, the building housing the Palmyra Historical Museum operated as a hotel and tavern. Facing the wrecking ball in the 1960s, the historical structure was saved and relocated to 123 Market Street in 1976. The museum is sited where the Breeden home burned to the ground. The family lost in the flames continue their existence, albeit in spirit, in the museum where 23 themed rooms display over 200 years of history and memorabilia related to the "Queen of Erie Canal towns."

The Wm. Phelps General Store once served as a boarding house, tavern, bakery and general store since its construction in 1826. William Phelps revamped the store fifty years later and resided upstairs with his family in their elegant home. His son, Julius left the store intact and ultimately locked the doors in 1940, leaving an incomparable time capsule. Sybil Phelps lived in the elegant home without electricity or indoor plumbing from 1875 until her passing in 1976! The spookiness is evident especially when Sybil manifests as a full-body apparition, the rarest and most spectacular supernatural display of them all! One employee who sighted the ghost said she told the worker not to touch her stuff. The worker replied, "No problem," and quickly exited the building.

An invisible presence is noticeable in every room. Whispers and footsteps are heard and some visitors feel the gentle touch from Holly, an 8-year-old, 19th century girl. The child often strokes or holds visitors' hands. She and several other spirit children like to hide under a chair-side table in the living room.

A large number of paranormal investigative groups experienced strange noises and captured spirit anomalies in photographs including the apparition of a young boy. Some lucky ones sighted the apparition of a little girl who appeared upstairs in the residence. A spectral black cat sometimes saunters through the store and walks up the stairs pausing only to rub against visitors' legs.

Every day is a supernatural adventure at the museum where staffers and volunteers lovingly acknowledge the spirits who stay-behind. They even hang Christmas stockings for the children every year.

The Children's Room is the most popular area in the museum. Filled with toys, the room hosts the spirits of the six children who perished in the fire. A tape recorder left running in the vacant room captured 45 minutes of the sounds of children playing with toys, even the distinctive sound of metal roller skates. Afterwards, nothing in the room looked out of place according to Bonnie Hays, Executive Director of Historic Palmyra.

Surveillance cameras are an invaluable resource for capturing ghostly antics. The lens recorded items moving, cupboards opening and doors closing. Most astonishing, the camera revealed a picture hanging in the Merchant Room, rise off its hook, lower to the floor and be placed in front of the door.

Regarded as "the most haunted place in the Finger Lakes," experience nighttime at the Wm. Phelps General Store and the Palmyra Historical Museum for their haunted history. Historic Palmyra offers unusual happenings and spirits in both buildings. Ghost hunting opportunities are available anytime throughout the year.

Seneca Falls Historical Museum

55 Cayuga Street

SENECA FALLS

The first women's rights convention in the United States took place at Seneca Falls in 1848 led by two New York residents, Susan B. Anthony and Elizabeth Cady Stanton. They appealed for women's right to vote, to be educated and to own property in their own names.

The Seneca Falls Historical Museum is housed in a 23-room Queen Anne Style mansion. Founded in 1896, women's history is the museum's focus. As you would expect, the museum provides equal opportunity to its phantom population providing a haven to spirits of both sexes.

Edward Mynderse, son of the early land developer Colonel Wilhelmus Mynderse, resided in the family domicile living off his inheritance until his death. When the Becker family moved in and remodeled the 1855 house, the renovation awakened Edward's sleeping spirit. Much like physical beings, spirits don't take kindly to change. Apparently Edward felt perturbed. Doors opened and closed on their own, unexplainable noises resounded, furnishings and paintings became rearranged, the china and silverware on the buffet rattled and clocks went cuckoo.

The museum staff welcomes Edward's spirit for they feel he watches over his mortal abode and the mortals who run it. Docents always acknowledge his presence and share stories of his antics, which include tossing stuffed animals and removing tacks from the storm window plastic.

Another spirit present in the house is a young Irish maid who died of consumption at 15-years-old. Staffers hear her crying on the back stairs, which are the ones she would have used. They swear someone is sobbing in the back only to find no one.

The Becker family lived in the grand home for 70 years and employed a nanny named Mary Merrigan. Quartered on the third floor, Mary delighted in make-believe and dressing the children in costumes. Ultimately, Mary began to suffer from dementia and the Beckers placed her in a rest home called the Willard State Hospital.

One evening, Mary showed up in the living room wearing her uniform. The Beckers sent her up to bed with the intention of returning her to the home the next day. When they went to rouse her in the morning her room stood empty and looked undisturbed. As they pondered this mystery the phone rang. The hospital called to inform the family Mary passed away the night before at 8:10 P.M., the *exact* time Mary appeared in the Becker's living room.

At one time, workmen got goose bumps when a ghostly maid and costumed lass showed up to watch them work.

In 2002, the historical society hosted a camera crew and a psychic medium for an overnight stay. Without knowledge of the paranormal events occurring in the house, the female medium couldn't sleep because three spirits kept her awake. She intuited the sobbing girl who wants to go home to Ireland. The group held a séance hoping to release the girl's spirit to the Other Side. The next year no one heard crying on the back stairs.

It's important to note the Seneca Falls Historical Society mansion is not a proverbial haunted house. The resident spirits do not frighten—they provide a certain comfort.

Snug Harbor

1000 Richmond Terrace
STATEN ISLAND

Before he died, Captain Robert Richard Randall retained Alexander Hamilton to establish a retirement home for "Aged, Decrepit, and Worn-out Sailors." A bachelor mariner himself, Randall aspired to create a safe harbor for retired seafarers. In 1833, the 14-acre Sailors' Snug Harbor opened on Staten Island.

The seamen's retirement campus became a world unto itself. Dormitories and dining halls existed in five Greek revival buildings. The property included the Randall Memorial Church and adjacent Music Hall, a large hospital and four-winged sanitarium, laundry, blacksmith's shop, farm buildings and a morgue. As the number of residents dwindled in the mid-20th century, the institution experienced financial difficulties. The once grand structures fell into disrepair; some were demolished including the domed church. In the 1960s, the New York City Landmarks Commission designated the remaining buildings as the city's first landmark structures and listed them on the National Register of Historic Places.

Today the stunning 83-acre park-like setting is home to the Snug Harbor Cultural Center & Botanical Garden, a leading venue for cultural entertainment. Snug Harbor offers a blend of gardens, museums, theaters, educational opportunities and seasonal festivals. Although no mortal sailors reside here today, their spirits do.

Matron's Cottage

When I asked a worker if she thought the cultural complex was haunted she quickly and unequivocally responded, "Of course it is. The park rangers feel them at night all the time; they feel the ghosts pass right through them. There's the "Old Matron," she began…

The Matron's Cottage housed unmarried, full-time, female employees. The women worked as seamstresses, cooks and washerwomen. The Matron was an educated woman who kept detailed records and directed the female staff. According to legend, one 19th century matron bore an illegitimate son who she kept hidden in the basement.

Around the age of 13, he escaped his confinement and murdered his mother. The Matron's specter appears in several locations across the campus. Rangers and other staffers report unusual happenings in the house. Doors constantly unlock by themselves, objects disappear only to reappear somewhere else and even what sounds like chains rattling in the basement.

Cited as Snug Harbor's most haunted building, the rumors attracted the The Atlantic Paranormal Society in 2011 to film a *Ghost Hunters* episode entitled "Murdered Matron." Team members heard a chair sliding and a barely audible voice in the residence. Astoundingly, the spirits engaged in a flashlight conversation. The spirits were asked questions and they responded by turning the flashlight on and off. Were they talking to the Matron? The spirit answered, "No."

Not all 900 resident "snugs" behaved well. One story concerns a mature, female worker who took a liking to one of the younger men. Her persistent attentions angered him so much he allegedly resorted to murder. Could she be the mysterious woman in white seen weeping by Cottage 3 who suddenly evaporates when offered assistance?

Then there's the charming "Old Salt," an elderly gent who is an authority on the complex's history. Most friendly and helpful, he can answer any question posed. In fact he'd make an excellent tour guide. One small problem—he's a ghost!

The Music Hall's grand architecture serves as the perfect setting for concerts, theater, lectures and ghosts!

What about the Music Hall ghost? This music aficionado prefers balcony seats and doors pose no boundaries to him—he walks right through them! When journalist and television personality Meredith Vieira teamed up with the *Ghost Hunters* to investigate the site, she spotted someone moving in the balcony. They all heard footsteps, giggling and a strange hooting sound echoing in the venue.

This cultural center is home to over twenty non-profit organizations and the address of earth bound spirit Thomas Melville, former governor of the institution and brother of Herman Melville author of *Moby Dick*. Who wouldn't want to stay anchored here amidst history, culture, classical architecture and beautiful botanical gardens?

Figments of the imagination? No way. Far too many witnessed oddities to doubt the reality of their experiences.

Another employee underwent a unique encounter. Her father loved walking the grounds and frequently visited. After his death, she shared memories of him with a co-worker. Suddenly, his signature scent, a mixture of Aqua Velva and Old Spice colognes, perfumed the atmosphere for about fifteen minutes.

A visit to this National Historic Landmark District is a must—the guides are out of this world.

Shoppes at the Finish Line

809 Court Street
UTICA

Founded in 1847, the Globe Woolen Company constructed their mill in Utica's west end brewery district during the height of the city's industrial growth. In 1855, the company became the Utica Woolen Mills and continued to thrive. In 1873, larger and improved buildings were erected and the business continued to operate until 1916 when the American Woolen Company purchased the enterprise.

When operations ceased in the 1950s, the buildings were repurposed for college classrooms and later as offices.

Today, Utica's Globe Mill is a National Registered Historic Place and houses the Shoppes at the Finish Line. A number of spirits call the landmark home as well. Ghost enthusiasts investigating the building experienced countless anomalies…

Tuning into the lingering spirts, psychic medium Bobbie Sharp Delucia identified one of the entities as a former foreman who oversaw operations during the mill's heyday. Most often his spirit is encountered when individuals visit the second floor. He seems to be irritated with others infringing on his space or perhaps he shows his displeasure because the people who are present are being unproductive? He may be taking his work way too seriously by choosing to stay behind.

There's also a spirit boy in residence. Ghost hunters recorded his voice many times during EVP sessions such as a little boy saying "Yeah." Some photos reveal a childlike figure as well. During a paranormal investigation a news reporter witnessed a boy's spirit and simultaneously received a scratch.

Sue Keller is the Property Manager and she feels the haunting activity seems to escalate between the hours of 4:00-5:00 P.M. She speculates since it's the traditional quitting time, the hour accounts for what sounds like people moving about upstairs. Visitors to the building at night, when the place is empty, often hear disembodied footsteps.

Among the odd noises, ethereal voices and sounds of moving furniture, even customers sighted shadow figures.

The mill possesses a tragic past which may account for the hauntings. In 1871, fire consumed the entire mill and its contents. A gruesome elevator accident occurred on-site when a worker got caught up in the mechanism's pulley system. The aforementioned foreman witnessed the mishap. No wonder he's grumpy.

Paranormal investigator Marcus Zwierecki seeking spirits in the Shoppes at the Finish Line.

Marcus Zwierecki, co-author of *Ghost Hunting the Mohawk Valley,* conducted paranormal classes at the venue. He heard furniture moving around on the vacant floor above either when alone or with others. Marcus observed shadow people in his peripheral vision and clearly heard ghostly voices call out, "Hey!" or "Over there!" when no one else was present.

A Spirit Box, also known as an Instrumental Trans Communications (ITC) box, is a device used for contacting spirits through the use of radio frequency. During a Spirit Box session, Marcus clearly heard a response to the question, "Do you know where you are?" The spirit answered, "In the mill." He also received responses from long-gone workers stating how they worked and how many worked with them.

Medical records are stored in the building and once a large quantity of them were found scattered about the floor. In this area, Marcus captured orbs in some photos, a white mist in others and one shot includes the spectral silhouette of a little boy.

Hidden underground waterways still flow through Utica. Nail Creek runs into West Utica where it once served as the main power source for the mill. The stream continues to silently run its course beneath the structure and at one time was navigable under the building. Running water can generate increased paranormal activity; ghosts draw energy from the water to manifest. When Sue, Bobbi and Marcus investigated the basement using an Ovilus (the Ovilus digitally produces preprogrammed words randomly generated by variations in magnetic fields), Bobbi felt extreme anxiety. The Ovilus generated the words, "Get out!"

Lights often turn on in the attic without benefit of human hand. Sometimes as people ascend the stairs to the top floor, they feel an unseen force preventing them from moving forward. Sue ensures the lights are turned off when leaving the building but there are times when she reaches the parking lot and sees the lights are blazing. Something remains very present in the old structure.

Many thanks to Sue Keller and
Marcus Zwierecki for serving up spirits.

Hotel Utica

102 Lafayette Street
UTICA

Hotel Utica's "Tuxedo Man" is the city's most famous ghost yet no one knows his identity. Several hotel guests glimpsed a man wearing a tuxedo who disappeared before their eyes. He is most often spotted at the bar enjoying a drink. The phantom moves objects, such as salt and pepper shakers and plates and sometimes breaks bottles. He wanders throughout the hotel, his presence gracing the ballroom and upper floor hallways. When noticed, he's in formal dress and usually talking.

Hotel Utica opened in 1912. At the time, the hotel ranked as one of the most luxurious hotels on the East Coast. Towering over downtown Utica, the inn is the city's crown jewel. Over its lifetime the hotel hosted celebrities and political figures including President William Taft, Franklin Delano and Eleanor Roosevelt and Amelia Earhart. Mickey Mantle and Jackie Robinson overnighted here en route to an All-Star baseball game in Cooperstown. During World War II, many movie stars and singers stayed at the hotel as they toured the country visiting injured soldiers. Rita Hayworth, Bobby Darin, Johnny Cash and Judy Garland are among the many notables. The guesthouse is listed with the National Trust Historic Hotels of America.

The hotel ceased operating in 1972 and sat vacant for a while. After extensive restoration, the hotel reopened in 2001. Some floors remain off-limits to the public and rumors persist departed guests still roam the halls.

Utica Hotel, Utica, N. Y.

Considering all the guests who passed through its doors, as in most vintage hotels, it's likely some guests never checked out. With all the galas and special events celebrated here, it is not surprising Hotel Utica is haunted. Several hotel staff members claim they've witnessed inexplicable happenings. The sound of phantom parties emanates from the ballroom, knocking noises and footsteps resound down vacant halls. A few report feeling uncomfortable in the stairwells.

Sometimes lobby chandeliers turn off for no reason. Some guests witnessed a diminutive, elderly housekeeper walking the halls in the wee hours; no housekeeping staff is on the scene at that time. There are also reports of an ethereal woman wearing a light-colored, 1920s era dress watching from the mezzanine when large parties are in full swing. Ghostly figures have been seen in the kitchen.

Staff members claim Room 410 is one of the most haunted chambers. During renovations the front desk received multiple calls from the unoccupied room and heard only static on the line. When the desk called the room "someone" answered the phone but again only static. In some paranormal experiments, when static noise is played at a slower speed, voices can be heard. To further the mystery, after multiple calls, staff investigated the room and discovered the phone unplugged. How is this even possible? Also, during this same time, the shower sometimes ran boiling hot on its own.

Rooms 408 and 409 are other haunted rooms. Sometimes guests feel compelled to vacate those places because they sense a presence and feel discomfort. Hotel Utica now hosts 4th floor ghost hunts.

Kris Williams of Syfy Channel's *Ghost Hunters* investigated Hotel Utica on Halloween 2015. Kris joined *Haunts & Legends LIVE*, along with Chris DiCesare of Syfy's *School Spirits* and the Shadow Chasers, in a first time investigation of the haunted hotel, including the forbidden 13th floor. After reviewing camera footage of the hunt, a ghostly face appeared and the team captured eerie voices as well. That same night, Utica resident Vicki Chwazik snapped a photo when something caught her eye. Astoundingly, the photo reveals a bearded man dressed in a cloak and top hat. No physical person matching this description attended the event so perhaps the photo is tangible evidence of Tuxedo Man.

U. S. Military Academy

WEST POINT

Superintendent's Quarters,
United States Military Academy at West Point.

Situated on high ground overlooking the Hudson River, West Point is the nation's oldest military post in continuous operation. General George Washington considered the imposing plateau fledgling America's most strategic location. He appointed Thaddeus Kosciusko, hero of Saratoga, to design the fortification in 1778.

During the Revolution, West Point served as Washington's headquarters. To safeguard the important waterway, an 150-ton iron chain was draped across the sharply angled river to Constitution Island, preventing passage by the British. The British, despite Benedict Arnold's betrayal, never captured the fortress.

The Academy traces its roots to 1801, when President Thomas Jefferson set plans in motion to establish the military school. A popular tourist destination, the campus is a national landmark featuring scores of historic sites, buildings and monuments complete with a large visitor center and museum.

Graduates serving under Generals Grant, Lee, Sherman and Jackson, set high standards of military leadership during the Civil War for both the North and South. Eisenhower, MacArthur, Bradley and Patton stand out as legendary USMA graduates who met the challenges of leadership in World War II. On the other hand, one-time cadets Edgar Allan Poe and James Whistler, opted for alternative careers.

Colonel Sylvanus Thayer, considered the "Father of the Military Academy," established the curriculum and served as superintendent from 1817–1833. The colonel's residence accommodates "Miss Molly's" spirit. Miss Molly served as Thayer's maid. The bed in the room where she used to sleep usually looks rumpled. Her spirit sometimes "borrows" guests' possessions, such as money and jewelry, and redeposits them in the master bedroom. Maybe Miss Molly resents the extra work caused by visitors in the house. One guest awoke during the night and saw a woman in a long white dress standing over his bed. As he watched in awe, the phantom female turned and disappeared through a closed door.

Miss Molly's spirit was also spotted kneading bread in the basement kitchen. Legend says when she died, a mysterious mark appeared on the breadboard without cause. Perhaps the possessive housekeeper left a physical sign signaling her forever presence. Clearly she wants to be noticed.

In the 1920s, two servants living in the old Morrison House, (Quarters 107B) on Professors' Row, became so frightened they ran screaming from their room in the middle of the night. The phantom pursuer who caused their terror was allegedly a professor's deceased wife. Allegedly the professor reneged on a promise to his dying wife and married her mother. Some say her spirit lingered showing her displeasure from beyond the grave.

The most documented case of paranormal activity occurred in 1972 when several cadets sighted the luminous apparition of a gaunt, Civil War era soldier. Wearing a frayed, full-dress coat consistent with a 19th century Cavalry fighter, the forlorn specter carried a musket when he materialized in Room 4714 in the 47th Division. The specter regarded the cadets then turned on his heels and walked through the wall. On a subsequent evening, upper-classmen slept in the room and they also felt an otherworldly presence. Astoundingly, the temperature of the room dropped from 27C to -18C. Officials hearing the account considered the academy's long-established Cadet Honor Code, which prohibits lying, and took the sightings seriously.

In 1972, paranormal investigators Ed and Lorraine Warren, visited West Point to lecture on the supernatural. During the visit the Warrens inspected the Superintendent's Quarters. Lorraine closed her eyes to tune-in and discerned the spirit presence of a 19th century soldier named Greer.

Old Fort Niagara

Scott Avenue

YOUNGSTOWN

S ituated on a bluff overlooking the Niagara River sits one of the oldest forts in the United States—a garrison once occupied by France, Great Britain, Canada and the United States at different times. The nation conquering this strategic location controlled access to the Great Lakes and the westward passage.

The French Castle is the stronghold's oldest structure and is built upon Fort Conti established here in 1678 by French explorer Robert de La Salle. Some historians claim the fort is constructed atop 2nd century structures when Native American tribes created one of twelve known forts, according to Mason Winfield's *Shadows of the Western Door.*

In 1759, during the French and Indian War, the garrison fell to the British until Americans conquered the battlement for the American revolutionaries. Soldiers fighting here during the War of 1812 witnessed one of the site's bloodiest events leaving more than 4,000 dead. A powder magazine caught fire and a 200 foot tower of flame shot into the air carrying debris and body fragments.

Old Fort Niagara's blood-soaked history accounts for its plethora of ghost activity. Reports of a headless apparition haunting the French Castle, unexplained shadows, slamming doors and mysterious light orbs are reported. These spooky accounts draw paranormal investigators including national ghost hunting shows like *Ghost Adventures, Ghost Lab* and *Ghost Hunters* to document activity.

In 1839, the first eerie tale appeared in print. The story goes that during a party held in the French Castle, two French officers, fueled by wine, quarreled over a Seneca maiden named Onita. Jean-Claude De Rochefort and Henri Le Clerc agreed on a swordfight to settle the contest and end the enmity. The ardent men dueled relentlessly, clash after clash. Finally, with a ghoulish flourish, De Rochefort savagely decapitated Le Clerc. LeClerc's bloody head rolled down the cobblestones and into a well.

The legend says on moonlit nights Le Clerc's headless apparition rambles about the French Castle and roams the battlements looking for his severed head. (Talk about losing your head over a woman…)

Another paranormal incident occurred in 1815 when a "hobgoblin," a countryside fairy, appeared in the cemetery. In the 1980s, a similar entity appeared on videotape as a filmy image.

Fort Niagara is noted as the most haunted site in Western New York. The paranormal reputation is bolstered by the sounds of disembodied footsteps, creaking doors, and "creepy" feelings experienced by staff and visitors. Overnighters experienced lucid dreams of 19th century activity. One reporter, who slept overnight at the site, discerned kitchen noises, chairs scraping the floorboards and soldiers marching.

Bibliography

Conley, Kirstan. "Albany's night-watchman 'hero' finally gets what he deserves." *New York Post*, July 27, 2017.

Eimbinder, Jerry. "Where the Ghosts Are." Tarrytown Patch.com, October 6, 2011.

Farnsworth, Cheri. *Haunted Hudson Valley*. Stackpole Books, 2010.

Hanley-Goff, M.J. "Ghost encounters with the Hudson Valley Paranormal Investigations." *Recordonline.com*. Retrieved 1 January 2018.

Hauck, Dennis William, *National Directory of Haunted Places*. Penguin Books, 1996.

Hawes, Jason. "Buyer Beware." *Ghost Hunters*, Syfy Channel, Season 8, Episode 2.

_____. "Too Many Apparitions in the Kitchen." *Ghost Hunters*, Syfy Channel, Season 10, Episode 2.

Holzer, Hans, *Ghosts, True Encounters with the World Beyond*. Black Dog & Levanthal Publishers, 1998.

Isenhart, Rebecca. "Hunting ghosts and history at the New York State Capitol." *Times Union*, October 27, 2009.

Jones, Louis C., *Things That Go Bump in the Night*. Syracuse University Press, 1983.

Lynn, Naomi. "Haunted Hotel Makes You Sign A Waiver Before You Stay." August 12, 2016. http://lite987.com/ny-haunted-hotel-waiver-before-stay/

Macken, Lynda Lee. *Empire Ghosts, New York State's Haunted Landmarks.* Black Cat Press, 2008.

_____. *Ghostly Gotham, New York City's Haunted History.* Black Cat Press, 2002.

_____. *Ghosts of Central New York.* Black Cat Press, 2009.

_____. *Haunted History of Staten Island.* Black Cat Press, 2000.

_____. *Haunted Houses of the Hudson Valley.* Black Cat Press, 2006.

_____. *Haunted Long Island.* Black Cat Press, 2004.

McConnell, Elaine. "Ghostly Apparitions at West Point." http://blog. usmalibrary.org/2014/10/30/ghostly-apparitions-at-west-point/

Mead, Robin, *Haunted Hotels.* Rutledge Hill Press, Nashville, TN; 1995.

Merritt, Jim, "Stalking Specters." *NEWSDAY*, October 29, 2000.

Moran, Michael & Scott, Beth, *Historic Haunted America.* Tor Books, 1995.

Nye, Phil. "The Forbidden Floors of Haunted Hotel Utica." May 28, 2015. http://lite987.com/the-forbidden-floors-of-haunted-hotel-utica-the-haunts-and-legends-of-new-york/

_____. "The 1890 House Museum Haunting In Cortland, NY." October 23, 2015. http://lite987.com/the-1890-house-museum-haunting-in-cortland-ny-cny-paranormal/

_____. "The Ghosts of Old Fort Niagara in Youngstown New York." January 8, 2015. http://lite987.com/the-ghosts-of-old-fort-niagara-in-youngstown-new-york-cny-paranormal/

_____. "Haunted Naples Hotel." May 31, 2013. http://lite987.com/haunted-naples-hotel-cny-paranormal-video/

_____. "The Haunting of the Historic Globe Mill." February 27, 2015. http://lite987.com/the-haunting-of-the-historic-globe-mill-cny-paranormal-video/

Pasko, Jessica. _____. "The Ghost of Eva Tanguay." October 20, 2009. http://alloveralbany.com/archive/2009/10/20/the-ghost-of-eva-tanguay

Pitkin, David J., *Ghosts of the Northeast.* Aurora Publications, 2002.

Randall, Monica. *Winfield, Living in the Shadows of the Woolworths*. Thomas Dunne Books, 2003.

Revai, Cherie. *The Big Book of New York Ghost Stories*. Stackpole Books, 2009.

Riservato, Rochelle. "Hudson Valley's Most Haunted." http://visitvortex.com/magazine/hudson-valleys-most-haunted

Schneider, Caitlin. "The Long, Haunted History of New York's Shanley Hotel." August 12, 2016. http://mentalfloss.com/article/84568/long-haunted-history-new-yorks-shanley-hotel

Smitten, Susan. *Ghost Stories of New York State*. Lone Pine Publishing International, 2004.

Strickler, Lon. "Paranormal Mysteries at White Inn." http://www.phantomsandmonsters.com/2010/03/paranormal-mysteries-at-white-inn.html

Taddeo, Sarah. "Spirits said to haunt Historic Naples Hotel." *Democrat & Chronicle*, October 2, 2015.

Whitacre, Tammy. "Boo! Spirits at home in Palmyra museums." *Finger Lakes Times*, October 29, 2017.

Wicker, Christine. *Lily Dale: The Town That Talks to the Dead*. Harper One, 2006.

Winfield, Mason. *Shadows of the Western Door*. Western New York Wares, 1997.

Zimmermann, Linda. *Ghost Investigator: Hauntings of the Hudson Valley, Volume 1*. Eagle Press, 2002.

WEBSITES

Atlas Obscura: www.atlasobscura.com

Belhurst Castle: www.belhurstcastle.com

Burn Brae Mansion: www.burnbraemansion.com

Dunkirk Lighthouse: www.dunkirklighthouse.com

Getting Curious about the Past: www.lihistory.com

Haunted History Trail of New York State: www.hauntedhistorytrail.com

Haunted New York: www.hauntedny.com

Hyde Hall: www.hydehall.org

Lily Dale Assembly: www.lilydaleassembly.com

Long Island Ghosts: www.hauntedlongisland.com

Naples Hotel: www.napleshotelny.com.

Newfane Historical Society: www.niagaracounty.org

New York State Assembly: www.assembly.state.ny.us

Old Fort Niagara: www.oldfortniagara.org

The Otesaga: www.otesaga.com

Seneca Falls Historical Society: www.sfhistoricalsociety.org

Shanley Hotel: www.shanleyhotel.com

U.S. Military Academy at West Point: www.usma.edu

The White Inn: www.whiteinn.com

Wikipedia: www.wikipedia.com

PHOTO CREDITS

Page x: Creative Commons Northeast tower of New York State Capitol framed by trees by Daniel Case is licensed under CC BY 3.0; page 3: Buffalo Central Terminal by Dave Pape; pages 6, 7, 58, 59, 106: Courtesy of the Library of Congress; page 9: Creative Commons Van Horn Mansion by Kdm85 is licensed under CC BY 3.0; page 15: Courtesy of the Cohoes Music Hall; page 16: Eva Tanguay, Billy Rose Theatre Collection, New York Public Library; page 18: Courtesy of the Otesaga Hotel; page 25: Point Gratiot Light by Pubdog; page 28: Creative Commons Snow-covered roof of Fire Island Lighthouse by dans362 is licensed under CC BY SA 3.0; page 33: Courtesy of Belhurst Castle; page 39: Courtesy of Burn Brae Mansion; page 46: Creative Commons Lindenwald NY by Acroterion is licensed under CC BY SA 4.0 Intl.; page 50: Courtesy of Lily Dale Assembly, Inc.; page 54: Angel House courtesy of TripAdvisor; page 63: Creative Commons WTM tony 0080 by Tony is licensed under CC BY SA 3.0; page 70: Red Coach Inn courtesy of TripAdvisor; page 72: Shutterstock; page 83: Phelps General Store courtesy of TripAdvisor; page 87: Courtesy of Seneca Falls Museum; page 89: Creative Commons NLN Matrons Cottage by Thomas Altfather Good is licensed under CC BY SA 4.0 Intl.; page 91: SH Music Hall shaded jeh by Jim Henderson; page 93: Globe Woolen Company Mills courtesy of the National Park Service; pages 95 & 97: Lorrie Hale; page 101: USMA Supe's Quarters by Ahodges7. All other photos by the author.

Enjoy more of Lynda Lee Macken's haunting titles…

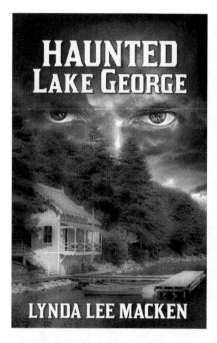

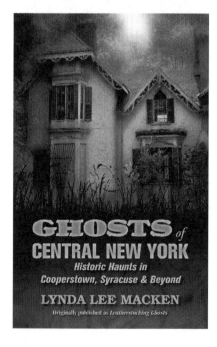

Made in the USA
Middletown, DE
20 August 2021

45492024R00071